Table of Contents
Introductory Algebra

Shape Patterns

Directions: Solve the pattern problems.

1. Draw the next three figures in the pattern. Describe the pattern.

2.

    a. Describe the pattern in the top row of numbers from one shape to the next.

    b. Describe the pattern in the bottom row of numbers from one shape to the next.

    c. Describe the pattern between the top and bottom numbers in each shape.

    d. Describe the shading pattern.

    e. Draw the next 3 figures in the pattern.

Expanding

 Draw a series of figures that have more than 1 pattern.

Function Machine

Directions: The function machine uses rules to change numbers.
Look for a pattern in the IN and OUT numbers in each table.
Fill in the table.
Write the rule.

1.

IN	2	4	7	8	9
OUT	10	20	35		

Rule: _____

2.

IN	30	40	45	50	55
OUT	6	8			

Rule: _____

Describing

Describe how the rules are alike and how the rules are different.

Number Patterns

Directions: Find the patterns in the table.

1. Look at the columns.

    a. Do the columns have a **growing pattern** or a **decreasing pattern**?

    b. Do the columns change at a **steady rate**?

    c. Write the rule for each column.

	C1	C2	C3	C4	C5	C6
R1	3	4	7	11	18	
R2	6	8	14	22	36	
R3	12	16	28	44	72	
R4	24	32	56	88	144	

2. Look at each row.

    a. Do the rows have a **growing pattern** or a **decreasing pattern**?

    b. Do the rows change at a **steady rate**?

    c. Describe the rule for each row.

3. Fill in the sixth column. How do you know you did this correctly?

Expanding

    Make a table that has a row pattern and a different column pattern.

Name _____

Who's Taller?

Directions: Solve the problems.

Danielle, Tamequa, Rashawn, and Joaquín have been good friends since kindergarten. Their heights changed a good deal over the years.

1. When they were in kindergarten, Danielle was taller than Rashawn but not Joaquín. Tamequa was taller than exactly two of the other children.

    a. Put the children in order from shortest to tallest.

    _____ _____ _____ _____

       shortest   tallest

    b. Explain how you found the answer.

Height

	1	2	3	4
Danielle				
Tamequa				
Rashawn				
Joaquín				

1 = shortest   4 = tallest

2. When they were in third grade, Joaquín was neither the shortest nor the tallest. Rashawn was shorter than Tamequa and Danielle. Danielle was shorter than Tamequa and Joaquín.

    a. Use the chart. Put an **x** in a space if the child cannot be that height. Put a circle in the space if the child must be that height.

    b. Put the children in order from shortest to tallest.

    _____ _____ _____ _____

       shortest   tallest

Organizing

Explain the method that helps you organize the clues the best.

All About Order

Directions: Solve the problems.

Danielle, Tamequa, Rashawn, and Joaquín are in Ms. Thompson's fifth-grade class. Use the clues and the logic charts to put the children in order from shortest to tallest and from youngest to oldest.

Clues:
Danielle is not the shortest child.
Rashawn is older than Tamequa and Joaquín.
The shortest child is also the oldest.
Joaquín is taller than exactly one other child.
Danielle is the only child to have the same ranking in both height and age.

Height

	1	2	3	4
Danielle				
Tamequa				
Rashawn				
Joaquín				

1 = shortest   4 = tallest

Age

	1	2	3	4
Danielle				
Tamequa				
Rashawn				
Joaquín				

1 = youngest   4 = oldest

shortest _____

_____

_____

tallest _____

youngest _____

_____

_____

oldest _____

Reflecting

Danielle is not the shortest. The shortest child is also the oldest. What do these two clues tell you about Danielle's age?

Missing Numbers

Directions: Solve the problems.

Symbols that are the same represent the same number.
Symbols that are different represent different numbers.

1. ♣ x ⭐ = 16.

   a. Find all the pairs of whole numbers that make the equation true.

   ♣ = _____   ⭐ = _____   ♣ = _____   ⭐ = _____

   ♣ = _____   ⭐ = _____   ♣ = _____   ⭐ = _____

   b. How do you know you found all possibilities?

   c. What is a name that describes all the numbers you found in part **a**? _____

2. ♦ ÷ ♥ = 6. Find at least 4 pairs of whole numbers that make the equation true.

   ♦ = _____   ♥ = _____

   ♦ = _____   ♥ = _____

   ♦ = _____   ♥ = _____

   ♦ = _____   ♥ = _____

Reflecting

Is it possible to find all possible whole numbers that make the equation in problem 2 true? Why or why not?

More Missing Numbers

Directions: Solve the problems.

Symbols that are the same represent the same number.
Symbols that are different represent different numbers.

1. ♣ + ♣ + ♣ = 27   ♣ = _____

2. ♦ + ♦ = 26   ♦ = _____

3. Is there more than one possible answer for ♣?
   For ♦? Explain.

4. ★ – ★ = ♥

   ★ = _____   ♥ = _____

5. ☺ ÷ ☺ = ✿

   ☺ = _____   ✿ = _____

Expanding

Try different values for ★. What do you notice about the value of ♥?

Try different values for ☺. What do you notice about the value of ✿?

Finding Unknowns

Directions: Find out how the children voted.

The fifth-grade classes voted on the location of their class trip. They could choose the beach, the amusement park, or the science museum.

B = beach   **A** = amusement park   **S** = science museum

Room 9:

12 votes for the beach
5 votes for the science museum
27 votes in all

B = _____   A = _____   S = _____

Room 10:

10 votes for the beach
3 times more votes for the amusement park than for the science museum
30 votes in all

B = _____   A = _____   S = _____

Room 11:

4 votes for the science museum
8 votes for the beach
$\frac{1}{2}$ as many votes for the beach as for the amusement park

_____ votes in all

B = _____   A = _____   S = _____

Explaining

Explain the strategies you used to find your answers.

Making Equations

Directions: Solve the problems.

1. Sandra gets a job babysitting for the Andersons. They pay her $4 per hour.

   a. How much will she make if she babysits for 3 hours? _____

   b. How much will she make if she babysits for 4 hours? _____

   c. Let **H** be the number of hours she works. Let **M** be the amount of money she makes. Write an equation.

   M = _____

2. Uyen's father is taking her and some friends to the movies for her birthday. Movie tickets cost $5 per child and $8 per adult.

   a. Uyen brings 4 friends. How much will the children's tickets cost?

   b. What will be the total cost of all the tickets (including Uyen's father)?

   c. What will be the total cost of all the tickets if Uyen brings 6 friends? Show your work.

   d. Let **T** be the number of children's tickets. Let **C** be the total cost of all the tickets.

   Write an equation. **C =** _____

Describing

Music lessons cost $10 per lesson. Let **L** be the number of lessons. Let **C** be the total cost. Write an equation. Describe the process you used to find the equation.

   C = _____

Show Me the Money!

Directions: Solve the problems.

Sara is 11 years old. Sara's grandmother offered to help pay for college. Her grandmother gave her two options.

Option 1: $1,000 each year on her birthday, ending on her eighteenth birthday.

Option 2: $100 on her twelfth birthday. Each birthday after that will be double the previous year's amount, ending on her eighteenth birthday.

1. Complete the table for option 1.

Birthday	12	13	14	15	16	17	18
Total Amt. Saved	1,000						

2. How much total money will Sara have saved for college

after her eighteenth birthday? _____

3. Describe the pattern in the table. How does Sara's fund grow?

Show Me the Money! (cont.)

4. Complete the table for option 2.

Birthday	12	13	14	15	16	17	18
Amt. Rcvd. Each Birthday	100	200					
Total Amt. Saved	100	300					

5. How much money will Sara have saved for college

after her eighteenth birthday? _____

6. Describe the pattern in the table. How does Sara's fund grow?

7. Which option should Sara choose? Why?

8. Should Sara's choice be different if the plan ends after her sixteenth birthday? Explain.

Comparing

Make a scatterplot for each option. Write a description comparing the graphs. What is different about how the savings grow? Does the amount of time the plan is in place make a difference in which option should be chosen?

Growing Patterns

Materials: tiles or cubes

Directions: Use tiles or cubes to make these shapes. Look for a pattern. Use the pattern to draw the next shape.

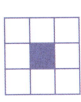 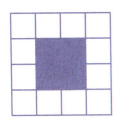 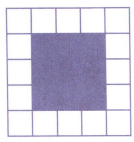

1. Describe the pattern.

2. Make a table.

Shape	1st	2nd	3rd	4th	5th
Number of Tiles	8	12	16		

3. How many tiles in the 10th shape? _____ The 15th? _____

Describing

 Describe how the pattern grows. Be specific.

Deep Blue Sea

An **integer** is any positive or negative whole number, or zero. Negative integers are numbers less than zero. The opposite of any number is found the same distance from 0 on a number line.

Example:

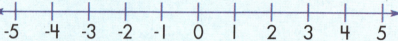

-5 -4 -3 -2 -1 0 1 2 3 4 5

35 below zero can be written as −35.
The opposite of 6 is −6.
The opposite of −41 is 41.
The opposite of 0 is 0.

Directions: Write a number for each description.

1. 5 feet below sea level _____

2. 14 degrees below zero _____

3. a loss of $10 _____

4. climbing down 9 feet into a cave _____

5. a 2-yard gain in a football game _____

6. 3 fewer fish than the day before _____

7. no change _____

8. driving a car 11 feet in reverse _____

Write a description for each integer.

−6 _____   −14 _____

−3 _____   −7 _____

0 _____   8 _____

4 _____   −4 _____

Write the opposite number.

6 _____   0 _____

4 _____   −14 _____

−9 _____   −7 _____

5 _____   25 _____

Weighing In

Example:

A number line can be used to compare integers. The farther to the right a number is, the greater it is.

3 is greater than −1.
2 is greater than −5.

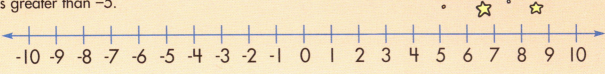

Directions: Circle the greater number in each pair.

Order in the Court

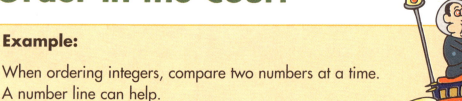

Example:

When ordering integers, compare two numbers at a time.
A number line can help.

-9 -8 -7 -6 -5 -4 -3 -2 -1 0 1 2 3 4 5 6 7 8 9

Put the numbers –4, 2, 0 in order from greatest to least.
–4 is less than 2.
2 is greater than 0.
0 is greater than –4.
2, 0, –4 shows the numbers in
order from greatest to least.

Directions: Write the numbers in order from least to greatest.

–6, 3, –2 _____ –6, –2, 3 _____   –4, –1, –2 _____

0, –3, 2 _____   7, –2, 4 _____

–3, –5, –1 _____   –2, –3, –6 _____

3, 7, 0 _____   1, 0, –1 _____

Directions: Write the numbers in order from greatest to least.

3, 0, 9 _____   –2, –3, 1 _____

–2, 5, 3 _____   2, 4, –3 _____

–4, 2, –3 _____   –4, –5, –1 _____

–2, –1, 0 _____   3, –2, 8 _____

Add Integers

A number line can be used to add integers.
To add positive integers, move to the right.
To add negative integers, move to the left.

Examples:

$4 + (-5) = (-1)$
Find 4 on the number
line. Move 5 spaces to the left.

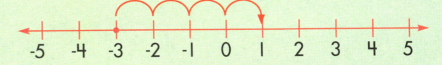

$(-3) + 4 = 1$

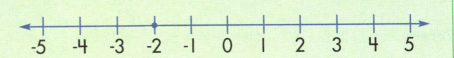

$(-2) + (-1) = (-3)$

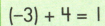

Directions: Add. Use the number lines to help you.

$2 + (-4) =$ _____

$(-3) + (-1) =$ _____

$(-1) + 4 =$ _____

$(-2) + 2 =$ _____

$4 + (-7) =$ _____

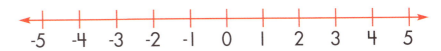

$0 + (-4) =$ _____

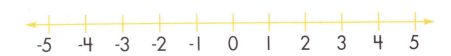

Subtract Integers

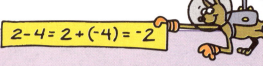

Steps:

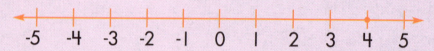

To subtract integers, change the subtraction problem to an addition problem. Then, change the second number in the problem to its opposite. (A –2 will be a 2; a 2 will be a –2.) Use a number line to solve the problem.

```
←——+——+——+——+——+——+——+——+——+——+——+——→
   -5  -4  -3  -2  -I   0   I   2   3   4   5
```

Examples:

$2 - 4 = 2 + (-4) = -2$ $3 - (-1) = 3 + 1 = 4$ $(-3) - 1 = (-3) + (-1) = -4$

$(-1) - (-3) = (-1) + 3 = 2$ $(-4) - (-4) = (-4) + 4 = 0$

Directions: Subtract. Show the addition problem that was used.

$1 - 5 =$ _____ $2 - (-2) =$ _____ $(-1) - (-6) =$ _____

$0 - 4 =$ _____ $(-1) - 2 =$ _____ $(-1) - (-1) =$ _____

$(-3) - (-5) =$ _____ $(-3) - 0 =$ _____ $4 - (-1) =$ _____

$2 - 3 =$ _____ $0 - (-2) =$ _____ $(-3) - 3 =$ _____

Directions: Write the **+** sign or **–** sign to make each problem true.

$-3 \;\square\; -2 = -5$ $1 \;\square\; 4 = -3$ $-1 \;\square\; -3 = 2$

$-2 \;\square\; -2 = 0$ $-4 \;\square\; 5 = 1$ $-3 \;\square\; -2 = -1$

Amazing Algebra

Directions: Find the value of the variable.

1. a x 51 = 2,601

a = _____

2. g ÷ 93 = 4

g = _____

3. 663 ÷ b = 3

b = _____

4. 61 x 19 = h

h = _____

5. 1,365 − c = 951

c = _____

6. 2i + 14 = 28

i = _____

7. 216 + 56 = d

d = _____

8. 30m − 600 = 300

m = _____

9. e x 42 = 1,008

e = _____

10. 1,249 − 75 = k

k = _____

Factoring Out

Directions: Find the prime factors of the members at the top of these graphic trees. The first one has been done for you.

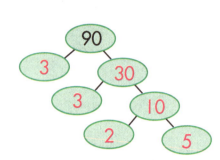

1.

2.

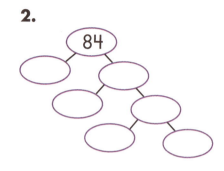

Prime Factors: _3, 3, 2, 5_

3 x 3 x 2 x 5 = 90

Prime Factors: _____

_____

Prime Factors: _____

_____

3.

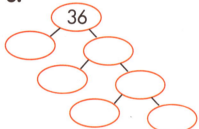

4.

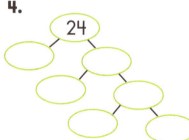

5.

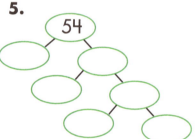

Prime Factors: _____

_____

Prime Factors: _____

_____

Prime Factors: _____

_____

6.

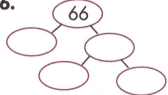

7.

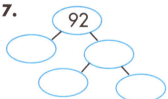

8.

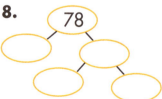

Prime Factors: _____

_____

Prime Factors: _____

_____

Prime Factors: _____

_____

Greatest Common Factors

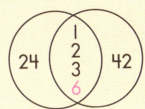

Two or more numbers can have common factors, or factors that are the same.

24: 1, 2, 3, 4, 6, 8, 12, 24
42: 1, 2, 3, 6, 7, 14, 21, 42

The common factors of 24 and 42 are 1, 2, 3, and 6.

The **greatest common factor** (GCF) is the largest factor shared by both numbers. The GCF of 24 and 42 is 6.

Examples: Find the GCF of 16, 28, and 56.

16: 1, 2, 4, 8, 16
28: 1, 2, 4, 7, 14, 28
56: 1, 2, 4, 7, 8, 14, 28, 56

The GCF of 16, 28, and 56 is 4.

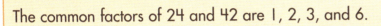
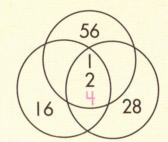

Directions: Find the greatest common factor (GCF) for each set of numbers.

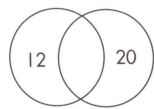
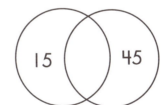
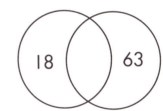

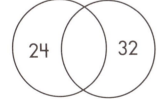
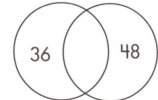
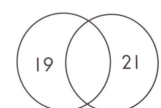

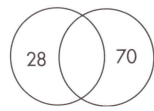
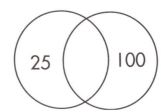
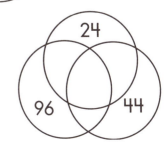

The Highest Peak

Directions: Find the greatest common factor (GCF) for each pair of numbers. Then, cross out one square at the bottom of the page that contains the answer. The letters to the remaining squares, written in order, will spell the answer to the following question:

What is the highest mountain peak in the world?

1. 12 and 30   GCF = _____   16 and 20   GCF = _____

2. 8 and 10   GCF = _____   7 and 9   GCF = _____

3. 6 and 12   GCF = _____   9 and 12   GCF = _____

4. 21 and 35   GCF = _____   10 and 16   GCF = _____

5. 12 and 18   GCF = _____   14 and 21   GCF = _____

6. 15 and 40   GCF = _____   36 and 48   GCF = _____

7. 16 and 24   GCF = _____   18 and 36   GCF = _____

8. 21 and 45   GCF = _____   24 and 42   GCF = _____

9. 18 and 30   GCF = _____   45 and 54   GCF = _____

10. 22 and 52   GCF = _____   16 and 64   GCF = _____

M	A	C	O	J	H	U	L
0	4	6	30	5	2	11	12
P	**N**	**Q**	**B**	**T**	**H**	**Y**	**E**
6	15	3	7	10	6	8	13
Z	**U**	**V**	**G**	**X**	**E**	**R**	**K**
18	7	22	3	1	20	14	6
F	**E**	**W**	**S**	**C**	**J**	**D**	**T**
2	17	6	21	9	2	16	25

___ ___ ___ ___ ___ ___   ___ ___ ___ ___ ___ ___ ___ ___ ___ ___

Least Common Multiples

The **least common multiple** (LCM) is the least multiple that a group of numbers has in common. The LCM helps when adding and subtracting fractions.

One way to find the LCM is to find the common multiples and choose the least one.

Example:

Multiples of 6: 6, 12, 18, 24, 30, 36, 42, 48, 54 . . .
Multiples of 9: 9, 18, 27, 36, 45, 54, 63, 72 . . .

Common multiples of 6 and 9 include 18, 36, and 54, but the least is 18.

Directions: Find the LCM for each set of numbers. The first one is done for you in the box at the bottom of the page.

8 and 3 ___24___   7 and 21 _____   5 and 8 _____   9 and 12 _____

6 and 16 _____   1 and 9 _____   4 and 7 _____   2 and 3 _____

10 and 4 _____   12 and 16 _____   6 and 8 _____   15 and 12 _____

2, 3, and 4 _____   3, 4, and 5 _____   2, 4, and 7 _____   3, 5, and 6 _____

Find two numbers that when multiplied together do not have a product of 30 but have a LCM of 30. _____

8   16   (24)   32   40   48   56   72   80

3   6   9   12   15   18   21   (24)   27

Name_____

The Factor and Multiple Trick

Directions: Find the greatest common factor (GCF) and the least common multiple (LCM) for each pair of numbers below. Next, find the product of the GCF and LCM and the product of the two numbers. What do you notice?

1.   **4, 6**

GCF   LCM

__2__   __12__

a. GCF x LCM = __24__

b. 4 x 6 = __24__

2.   **6, 9**

GCF   LCM

_____   _____

a. GCF x LCM = _____

b. 6 x 9 = _____

3.   **5, 15**

GCF   LCM

_____   _____

a. GCF x LCM = _____

b. 5 x 15 = _____

4.   **10, 12**

GCF   LCM

_____   _____

a. GCF x LCM = _____

b. 10 x 12 = _____

5.   **9, 12**

GCF   LCM

_____   _____

a. GCF x LCM = _____

b. 9 x 12 = _____

6.   **12, 18**

GCF   LCM

_____   _____

a. GCF x LCM = _____

b. 12 x 18 = _____

7.   **6, 8**

GCF   LCM

_____   _____

a. GCF x LCM = _____

b. 6 x 8 = _____

8.   **8, 20**

GCF   LCM

_____   _____

a. GCF x LCM = _____

b. 8 x 20 = _____

9.   **9, 24**

GCF   LCM

_____   _____

a. GCF x LCM = _____

b. 9 x 24 = _____

What did you notice about A and B?_____

My Dear Aunt Sally

Example:

To solve a problem with several operations, follow the rules of My Dear Aunt Sally.

My Dear = **M**ultiplication/**D**ivision

Aunt Sally = **A**ddition/**S**ubtraction

Do all multiplication and division steps first, in order from left to right. Then, do all addition and subtraction steps, in order from left to right.

These rules are called the Order of Operations.

$4 \times 8 + 36 \div 6 - 7$

$32 + 6 - 7$

$38 - 7$

31

Directions: Follow the Order of Operations to solve.

$4 + 5 \times 3 - 6 =$ _____

$4 - 3 + 6 \div 2 + 4 \times 2 =$ _____

$8 \div 4 + 3 \times 2 + 2 =$ _____

$5 \times 2 - 3 + 5 - 6 \div 3 =$ _____

$2 + 3 \times 2 - 4 + 2 \times 2 =$ _____

$6 - 2 + 3 - 2 \times 4 + 3 =$ _____

$4 \times 5 - 8 \div 2 + 5 \times 2 =$ _____

$9 \div 3 + 5 - 4 \div 2 + 6 =$ _____

$3 \times 3 + 3 - 3 \times 3 - 3 =$ _____

$8 - 4 \div 4 + 2 \times 3 - 2 =$ _____

Exciting Exponents

Directions: When you see a figure like 5^2, the 2 is the exponent and the 5 is the base. This means that the 5 is multiplied by itself two times. Fill in the crossword with solutions written in word form.

Across

1. $6^2 + 4 =$ _____

2. $4^2 - 2 =$ _____

3. $2^2 + 7 =$ _____

Down

1. $8^2 - 14 =$ _____

2. $4^2 \div 4 =$ _____

3. $7^2 + 11 =$ _____

4. $3^2 - 6 =$ _____

5. $20^2 - 399 =$ _____

Order of Operations Practice

Directions: Follow the order of operations to solve the number sentences below. Match each number sentence with its solution in the column on the right. Use the letters that correspond with each numbered problem to read the coded message.

_____ 1. $15 - (4 + 7)$

_____ 2. $5 \times 2^3 - (27 - 21)$

_____ 3. $8 + 6 \times 4 \div 8 - 5$

_____ 4. $3^3 \div (3 \times 3)$

_____ 5. $9 + 7 - 5 \times 3 + 10$

_____ 6. $32 \div 4 + 4 \times 3$

_____ 7. $3 + 4^3 - 7 \times 6$

_____ 8. $28 + (97 - 3^4) - 5 \times 7$

_____ 9. $90 \div 5 \times 2 + 16$

_____ 10. $5^3 - 84 \div 12 - (6 \times 3)$

_____ 11. $98 \div (15 - 8) \times 12$

_____ 12. $67 + 6^2 \times 6 \div (2 + 1)$

_____ 13. $114 - 16 \times 3 + 27 - 4$

_____ 14. $8^2 - (2 + 6 \times 4)$

A. 25	
B. 2	
C. 52	
D. 4	
E. 168	
F. 19	
G. 100	
H. 9	
I. 89	
J. 18	
K. 43	
L. 11	
M. 38	
N. 139	
O. 34	
P. 360	
Q. 317	
R. 6	
S. 20	
T. 3	
U. 36	
V. 98	
W. 10	
X. 206	
Y. 27	
Z. 32	

$\overline{10}\ \overline{2}\ \overline{2}\ \overline{1}\quad \overline{1}\ \overline{3}\ \overline{13}\ \overset{V}{\overline{11}}\ \overline{3}\ \overline{6}\quad \overline{7}\ \overline{12}\ \overline{1}\quad \overline{10}\ \overline{2}\ \overline{2}\ \overline{1}$

$\overline{14}\ \overline{7}\ \overline{4}\ \overline{8}\ \overline{11}\ \overline{14}\ \overline{7}\ \overline{4}\ \overline{13}\ \overline{9}\ \overline{13}\ \overline{7}\ \overline{12}\ \overline{6}\quad \overline{14}\ \overline{7}\ \overline{6}\ \overline{4}\ \overline{11}\ \overline{3}$

$\overline{4}\ \overline{8}\ \overline{11}\quad \overset{U}{\overline{3}}\quad \overline{5}\ \overline{11}\ \overline{6}\quad \overset{F}{\overline{2}}\quad \overline{4}\ \overline{8}\ \overline{11}\quad \overline{3}\ \overline{2}\ \overline{7}\ \overline{1}.$

Order Up!

Name _____

Directions: Complete the equations below, making sure you follow the order of operations.

> **1.** First, do parentheses, then brackets.
> **2.** Next, do multiplication and division, in order from left to right.
> **3.** Finally, do addition and subtraction, in order from left to right.

1. $35 + 50 + \frac{25}{5} \cdot 5 - (8 + 11) =$ _____

2. $-16 + (20 \cdot 6) \div (6 + 2) + 31 =$ _____

3. $3 \cdot 2 [4 + (9 \div 3)] =$ _____

4. $2 + [48 \div (12 + 4)] - 16 =$ _____

5. $2[-6(3 - 12) - 17] =$ _____

6. $\frac{1}{2} (-16 - 4) =$ _____

7. $50 \div [(4 \cdot 5) - (36 \div 2)] + -91 =$ _____

8. $[5(20 - 2)] \div \frac{30}{2} + 6 - 3 =$ _____

Shape Patterns

Directions: Solve the pattern problems. Draw the next three figures in the pattern. Describe the pattern.

1.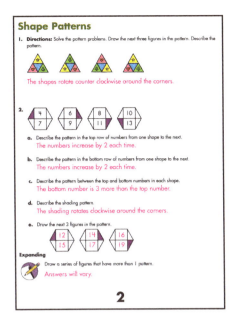

The shapes rotate counter clockwise around the corners.

2.
   a. Describe the pattern in the top row of numbers from one shape to the next.
   The numbers increase by 2 each time.
   b. Describe the pattern in the bottom row of numbers from one shape to the next.
   The numbers increase by 2 each time.
   c. Describe the pattern between the top and bottom numbers in each shape.
   The bottom number is 3 more than the top number.
   d. Describe the shading pattern.
   The shading rotates clockwise around the corners.
   e. Draw the next 3 figures in the pattern.
   12/15 14/17 16/19

Expanding

Draw a series of figures that have more than 1 pattern.
Answers will vary.

2

Function Machine

Directions: The function machine uses rules to change numbers. Look for a pattern in the IN and OUT numbers in each table. Fill in the table. Write the rule.

1.

IN	2	4	7	8	9
OUT	10	20	35	40	45

Rule: OUT = IN x 5

2.

IN	30	40	45	50	55
OUT	6	8	9	10	11

Rule: OUT = IN ÷ 5

Describing

Describe how the rules are alike and how the rules are different.
The rules are inverses of one another. They both use the number 5, but one is multiplication and the other is division.

3

Number Patterns

Directions: Find the patterns in the table.

1. Look at the columns.

	C1	C2	C3	C4	C5	C6
R1	3	4	7	11	18	29
R2	6	8	14	22	36	58
R3	12	16	28	44	72	116
R4	24	32	56	88	144	232

   a. Do the columns have a **growing pattern** or a **decreasing pattern**?
   growing pattern
   b. Do the columns change at a **steady rate**?
   no
   c. Write the rule for each column.
   All the columns have the rule x 2.

2. Look at each row.
   a. Do the rows have a **growing pattern** or a **decreasing pattern**?
   growing pattern
   b. Do the rows change at a **steady rate**?
   no
   c. Describe the rule for each row.
   Add the previous two numbers to get the next number.

3. Fill in the sixth column. How do you know you did this correctly?

Expanding

Make a table that has a row pattern and a different column pattern.
Answers will vary.

4

Who's Taller?

Directions: Solve the problems. Danielle, Tamequa, Rashawn, and Joaquin have been good friends since kindergarten. Their heights changed a good deal over the years.

1. When they were in kindergarten, Danielle was taller than Rashawn but not Joaquin. Tamequa was taller than exactly two of the other children.
   a. Put the children in order from shortest to tallest.

   Rashawn   Danielle   Tamequa   Joaquin
   shortest   tallest

   b. Explain how you found the answer.   Answers will vary. Tamequa must be third in height, since she is taller than exactly 2 of the children. Since Danielle is taller than Rashawn but not Joaquin, Rashawn must be shortest, Danielle must be the next shortest, and Joaquin must be the tallest.

2. When they were in third grade, Joaquin was neither the shortest nor the tallest. Rashawn was shorter than Tamequa and Danielle. Danielle was shorter than Tamequa and Joaquin.

   a. Use the chart. Put an **x** in a space if the child cannot be that height. Put a circle in the space if the child must be that height.

   Height

	1	2	3	4
Danielle	X	X	X	X
Tamequa	X	X	X	O
Rashawn	O	X	X	X
Joaquin	X	X	O	X

   1 = shortest   4 = tallest

   b. Put the children in order from shortest to tallest.

   Rashawn   Danielle   Joaquin   Tamequa
   shortest   tallest

Organizing

Explain the method that helps you organize the clues the best.
Answers will vary.

5

All About Order

Directions: Solve the problems. Danielle, Tamequa, Rashawn, and Joaquin are in Ms. Thompson's fifth-grade class. Use the clues and the logic charts to put the children in order from shortest to tallest and from youngest to oldest.

Clues:
Danielle is not the shortest child.
Rashawn is older than Tamequa and Joaquin.
The shortest child is also the oldest.
Joaquin is taller than exactly one other child.
Danielle is the only child to have the same ranking in both height and age.

Height

	1	2	3	4
Danielle	X	X	O	X
Tamequa	X	X	X	O
Rashawn	O	X	X	X
Joaquin	X	O	X	X

1 = shortest   4 = tallest

shortest   Rashawn
           Joaquin
           Danielle
tallest   Tamequa

Age

	1	2	3	4
Danielle	X	X	O	X
Tamequa	X	O	X	X
Rashawn	X	X	X	O
Joaquin	O	X	X	X

1 = youngest   4 = oldest

youngest   Joaquin
           Tamequa
           Danielle
oldest   Rashawn

Reflecting

Danielle is not the shortest. The shortest child is also the oldest. What do these two clues tell you about Danielle's age?
Danielle is not the oldest.

6

Missing Numbers

Directions: Solve the problems. Symbols that are the same represent the same number. Symbols that are different represent different numbers.

1. ♣ x ★ = 16.
   a. Find all the pairs of whole numbers that make the equation true.

   ♣ = 1   ★ = 2   ♣ = 16   ★ = 8
   ♣ = 16   ★ = 8   ♣ = 1   ★ = 2

   b. How do you know you found all possibilities?   Answers will vary.
   c. What is a name that describes all the numbers you found in part a?   factors of 16

2. ♦ + ♥ = 6. Find at least 4 pairs of whole numbers that make the equation true.
   Possible answers: There are multiple answers.

   ♦ = 12   ♥ = 2
   ♦ = 18   ♥ = 3
   ♦ = 24   ♥ = 4
   ♦ = 30   ♥ = 5

Reflecting

Is it possible to find all possible whole numbers that make the equation in problem 2 true? Why or why not?
No. There are an infinite number of solutions.

7

More Missing Numbers

Directions: Solve the problems. Symbols that are the same represent the same number. Symbols that are different represent different numbers.

1. ♣ + ♣ + ♣ = 27   ♣ = 9

2. ♦ + ♦ = 26   ♦ = 13

3. Is there more than one possible answer for ♣?   No.
   For ♦? Explain.

4. ★ – ★ = ♥   Answers will vary.
   Example:
   ★ = 8   ♥ = 0

5. ☺ ÷ ☺ = ✿   Answers will vary.
   Example:
   ☺ = 9   ✿ = 1

Expanding

Try different values for ★. What do you notice about the value of ♥?
Try different values for ☺. What do you notice about the value of ✿?
No matter what values you use for the star, the heart will always be 0.
No matter what values you use for the smiley face, the flower will always be 1.

8

Finding Unknowns

Directions: Find out how the children voted. The fifth-grade classes voted on the location of their class trip. They could choose the beach, the amusement park, or the science museum.

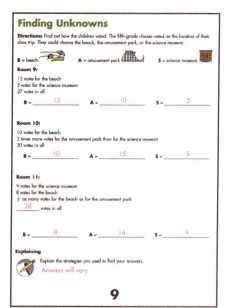

B = beach   A = amusement park   S = science museum

Room 9:

12 votes for the beach
5 votes for the science museum
27 votes in all

B = ___12___   A = ___10___   S = ___5___

Room 10:

10 votes for the beach
3 times more votes for the amusement park than for the science museum
30 votes in all

B = ___10___   A = ___15___   S = ___5___

Room 11:

4 votes for the science museum
8 votes for the beach
½ as many votes for the beach as for the amusement park
___28___ votes in all

B = ___8___   A = ___16___   S = ___4___

Explaining

Explain the strategies you used to find your answers.
Answers will vary.

9

Making Equations

Directions: Solve the problems.

1. Sandra gets a job babysitting for the Andersons. They pay her $4 per hour.
   a. How much will she make if she babysits for 3 hours? ___$12___
   b. How much will she make if she babysits for 4 hours? ___$16___
   c. Let **H** be the number of hours she works. Let **M** be the amount of money she makes. Write an equation.
   M = ___$4 × H___

2. Uyen's father is taking her and some friends to the movies for her birthday. Movie tickets cost $5 per child and $8 per adult.
   a. Uyen brings 4 friends. How much will the children's tickets cost? ___$25___
   b. What will be the total cost of all the tickets (including Uyen's father)? ___$33___
   c. What will be the total cost of all the tickets if Uyen brings 6 friends? Show your work. 7 × $5 + $8 = $43
   d. Let **T** be the number of children's tickets. Let **C** be the total cost of all the tickets. Write an equation. C = ___$5 × T + $8___

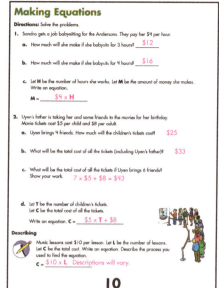

Describing

Music lessons cost $10 per lesson. Let **L** be the number of lessons. Let **C** be the total cost. Write an equation. Describe the process you used to find the equation.
C = ___$10 × L___ Descriptions will vary.

10

Show Me the Money!

Directions: Solve the problems. Sara is 11 years old. Sara's grandmother offered to help pay for college. Her grandmother gave her two options.

Option 1: $1,000 each year on her birthday, ending on her eighteenth birthday.

Option 2: $100 on her twelfth birthday. Each birthday after that will be double the previous year's amount, ending on her eighteenth birthday.

1. Complete the table for option 1.

Birthday	12	13	14	15	16	17	18
Total Amt. Saved	1,000	2,000	3,000	4,000	5,000	6,000	7,000

2. How much total money will Sara have saved for college after her eighteenth birthday? ___$7,000___

3. Describe the pattern in the table. How does Sara's fund grow?
Sara's fund grows $1,000 each year, which is a steady rate.

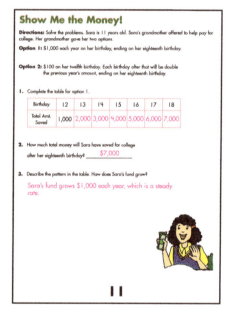

11

Show Me the Money! (cont.)

4. Complete the table for option 2.

Birthday	12	13	14	15	16	17	18
Amt. Rcvd. Each Birthday	100	200	400	800	1,600	3,200	6,400
Total Amt. Saved	100	300	700	1,500	3,100	6,300	12,700

5. How much money will Sara have saved for college after her eighteenth birthday? ___$12,700___

6. Describe the pattern in the table. How does Sara's fund grow?
The money grows slowly at first and then more rapidly. It grows at an increasing rate.

7. Which option should Sara choose? Why?
Sara will have more money for college if she chooses option 2.

8. Should Sara's choice be different if the plan ends after her sixteenth birthday? Explain.
If the plan ended after her sixteenth birthday, she should choose option 1. She would have $5,000 with option 1 and only $3,100 with option 2.

Comparing Option 1 grows at a steady rate. Option 2 grows at an increasing rate. The amount of time the plan is in effect does make a difference. Sara will have more money saved with option 1 up until her sixteenth birthday. After her seventeenth birthday, option 2 will be slightly higher. After her eighteenth birthday, option 2 gives her a much higher amount.

12

Growing Patterns

Materials: tiles or cubes

Directions: Use tiles or cubes to make these shapes. Look for a pattern. Use the pattern to draw the next shape.

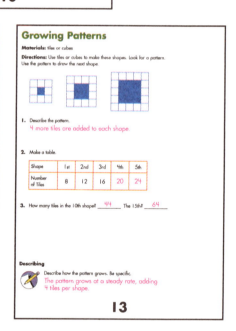

1. Describe the pattern.
4 more tiles are added to each shape.

2. Make a table.

Shape	1st	2nd	3rd	4th	5th
Number of Tiles	8	12	16	20	24

3. How many tiles in the 10th shape? ___44___ The 15th? ___64___

Describing

Describe how the pattern grows. Be specific.
The pattern grows at a steady rate, adding 4 tiles per shape.

13

Deep Blue Sea

An **integer** is any positive or negative whole number, or zero. Negative integers are numbers less than zero. The opposite of any number is found the same distance from 0 on a number line.

Example:

-5 -4 -3 -2 -1 0 1 2 3 4 5

35 below zero can be written as –35.
The opposite of 6 is –6.
The opposite of –41 is 41.
The opposite of 0 is 0.

Directions: Write a number for each description.

1. 5 feet below sea level ___–5___
2. 14 degrees below zero ___–14___
3. a loss of $10 ___–$10___
4. climbing down 9 feet into a cave ___–9___
5. a 2-yard gain in a football game ___+2___
6. 3 fewer fish than the day before ___–3___
7. no change ___0___
8. driving a car 11 feet in reverse ___–11___

Write a description for each integer. Descriptions will vary.

–6 feet below ground   –14 feet below sea level
–3 3 degrees below zero   –7 degrees colder than last night
0 no change   8 degrees above zero
4 foot high tree   –4 eggs less collected today

Write the opposite number.

6 ___–6___   0 ___same___
4 ___–4___   –14 ___14___
–9 ___9___   –7 ___7___
5 ___–5___   25 ___–25___

14

Weighing In

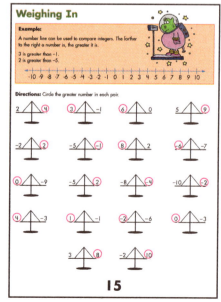

Example:

A number line can be used to compare integers. The farther to the right a number is, the greater it is.

3 is greater than –1.
2 is greater than –5.

-10 -9 -8 -7 -6 -5 -4 -3 -2 -1 0 1 2 3 4 5 6 7 8 9 10

Directions: Circle the greater number in each pair.

2 / ④   ③ / –1   ⑥ / 0   5 / ⑨

–2 / ②   –5 / ⑩   ⑧ / 2   ⑥ / –7

⓪ / –9   –5 / ②   –8 / ④   –10 / ②

④ / –3   ① / –1   –2 / ⑥   ⓪ / –3

3 / ⑧   –2 / ⑩

15

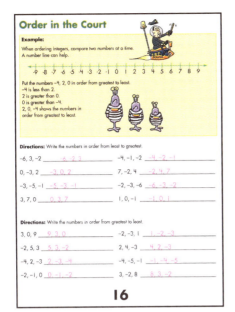

Order in the Court

Example:
When ordering integers, compare two numbers at a time.
A number line can help.

Put the numbers –4, 2, 0 in order from greatest to least.
–4 is less than 2.
2 is greater than 0.
0 is greater than –4.
2, 0, –4 shows the numbers in order from greatest to least.

Directions: Write the numbers in order from least to greatest.

–6, 3, –2 _____ –6, –2, 3 _____ –4, –1, –2 _____ –4, –2, –1
0, –3, 2 _____ –3, 0, 2 _____ 7, –2, 4 _____ –2, 4, 7
–3, –5, –1 _____ –5, –3, –1 _____ –2, –3, –6 _____ –6, –3, –2
3, 7, 0 _____ 0, 3, 7 _____ 1, 0, –1 _____ –1, 0, 1

Directions: Write the numbers in order from greatest to least.

3, 0, 9 _____ 9, 3, 0 _____ –2, –3, 1 _____ 1, –2, –3
–2, 5, 3 _____ 5, 3, –2 _____ 2, 4, –3 _____ 4, 2, –3
–4, –2, –3 _____ –2, –3, –4 _____ –4, –5, –1 _____ –1, –4, –5
–2, –1, 0 _____ 0, –1, –2 _____ 3, –2, 8 _____ 8, 3, –2

16

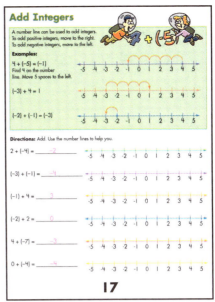

Add Integers

A number line can be used to add integers.
To add positive integers, move to the right.
To add negative integers, move to the left.

Examples:
4 + (–5) = (–1)
Find 4 on the number line. Move 5 spaces to the left.

(–3) + 4 = 1

(–2) + (–1) = (–3)

Directions: Add. Use the number lines to help you.

2 + (–4) = _____ –2
(–3) + (–1) = _____ –4
(–1) + 4 = _____ 3
(–2) + 2 = _____ 0
4 + (–7) = _____ –3
0 + (–4) = _____ –4

17

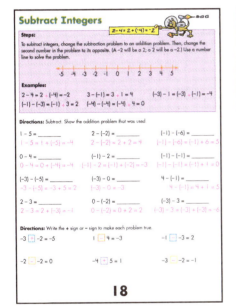

Subtract Integers

$2 - 4 = 2 + (-4) = -2$

Steps:
To subtract integers, change the subtraction problem to an addition problem. Then, change the second number in the problem to its opposite. (A –2 will be a 2, a 2 will be a –2.) Use a number line to solve the problem.

Examples:
2 – 4 = 2 + (–4) = –2   3 – (–1) = 3 . 1 = 4   (–3) – 1 = (–3) . (–1) = –4
(–1) – (–3) = (–1) . 3 = 2   (–4) – (–4) = (–4) . 4 = 0

Directions: Subtract. Show the addition problem that was used.

1 – 5 = _____
1 – 5 = 1 + (–5) = –4

2 – (–2) = _____
2 – (–2) = 2 + 2 = 4

(–1) – (–6) = _____
(–1) – (–6) = (–1) + 6 = 5

0 – 4 = _____
0 – 4 = 0 + (–4) = –4

(–1) – 2 = _____
(–1) – 2 = (–1) + (–2) = –3

(–1) – (–1) = _____
(–1) – (–1) = (–1) + 1 = 0

(–3) – (–5) = _____
–3 – (–5) = –3 + 5 = 2

(–3) – 0 = _____
(–3) – 0 = –3

4 – (–1) = _____
4 – (–1) = 4 + 1 = 5

2 – 3 = _____
2 – 3 = 2 + (–3) = –1

0 – (–2) = _____
0 – (–2) = 0 + 2 = 2

(–3) – 3 = _____
(–3) – 3 = (–3) + (–3) = –6

Directions: Write the + sign or – sign to make each problem true.

–3 $\boxed{+}$ –2 = –5   1 $\boxed{-}$ 4 = –3   –1 $\boxed{-}$ –3 = 2
–2 $\boxed{-}$ –2 = 0   –4 $\boxed{+}$ 5 = 1   –3 $\boxed{-}$ –2 = –1

18

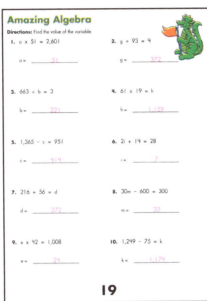

Amazing Algebra

Directions: Find the value of the variable.

1. a × 51 = 2,601
   a = _____ 51

2. g ÷ 93 = 4
   g = _____ 372

3. 663 ÷ b = 3
   b = _____ 221

4. 61 × 19 = h
   h = _____ 1,159

5. 1,365 – c = 951
   c = _____ 414

6. 2i + 14 = 28
   i = _____ 7

7. 216 + 56 = d
   d = _____ 272

8. 30m – 600 = 300
   m = _____ 30

9. e × 42 = 1,008
   e = _____ 24

10. 1,249 – 75 = k
    k = _____ 1,174

19

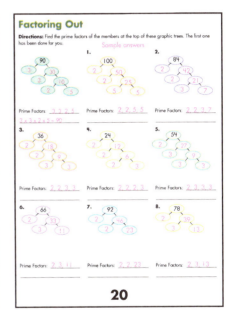

Factoring Out

Directions: Find the prime factors of the members at the top of these graphic trees. The first one has been done for you. Sample answers

1. 90 — Prime Factors: 3, 3, 2, 5
   2 × 3 × 2 × 5 = 90

1. 100 — Prime Factors: 2, 2, 5, 5

2. 84 — Prime Factors: 2, 2, 3, 7

3. 36 — Prime Factors: 2, 2, 3, 3

4. 24 — Prime Factors: 2, 2, 2, 3

5. 54 — Prime Factors: 2, 3, 3, 3

6. 66 — Prime Factors: 2, 3, 11

7. 92 — Prime Factors: 2, 2, 23

8. 78 — Prime Factors: 2, 3, 13

20

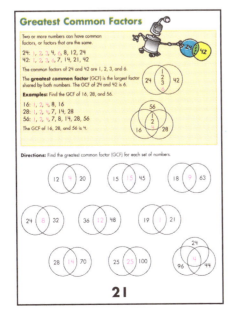

Greatest Common Factors

Two or more numbers can have common factors, or factors that are the same.
24: 1, 2, 3, 4, 6, 8, 12, 24
42: 1, 2, 3, 6, 7, 14, 21, 42
The common factors of 24 and 42 are 1, 2, 3, and 6.
The **greatest common factor** (GCF) is the largest factor shared by both numbers. The GCF of 24 and 42 is 6.

Examples: Find the GCF of 16, 28, and 56.
16: 1, 2, 4, 8, 16
28: 1, 2, 4, 7, 14, 28
56: 1, 2, 4, 7, 8, 14, 28, 56
The GCF of 16, 28, and 56 is 4.

Directions: Find the greatest common factor (GCF) for each set of numbers.

12 (4) 20   15 (15) 45   18 (9) 63
24 (8) 32   36 (12) 48   19 (1) 21
28 (14) 70   25 (25) 100   24, 96, 44 (4)

21

The Highest Peak

Directions: Find the greatest common factor (GCF) for each pair of numbers. Then, cross out one square at the bottom of the page that contains the answer. The letters to the remaining squares, written in order, will spell the answer to the following question:

What is the highest mountain peak in the world?

1. 12 and 30 GCF = 6   16 and 20 GCF = 4
2. 8 and 10 GCF = 2   7 and 9 GCF = 1
3. 6 and 12 GCF = 6   9 and 12 GCF = 3
4. 21 and 35 GCF = 7   10 and 16 GCF = 2
5. 12 and 18 GCF = 6   14 and 21 GCF = 7
6. 15 and 40 GCF = 5   36 and 48 GCF = 12
7. 16 and 24 GCF = 8   18 and 36 GCF = 18
8. 21 and 45 GCF = 3   24 and 42 GCF = 6
9. 18 and 30 GCF = 6   45 and 54 GCF = 9
10. 22 and 52 GCF = 2   16 and 64 GCF = 16

M	A	C	O	J	S	H	U	L
0	4	6	30	5	2	11	12	
P	**N**	**Q**	**B**	**T**	**H**	**Y**	**E**	
6	15	3	7	10	8	13		
Z	**U**	**V**	**G**	**X**	**E**	**R**	**K**	
18	7	22	3	1	20	14	9	
F	**E**	**W**	**S**	**J**	**D**	**T**		
2	17	6	21	9	2	16	25	

M O U N T   E V E R E S T

22

Least Common Multiples

The **least common multiple** (LCM) is the least multiple that a group of numbers has in common. The LCM helps when adding and subtracting fractions.

One way to find the LCM is to find the common multiples and choose the least one.

Example:
Multiples of 6: 6, 12, 18, 24, 30, 36, 42, 48, 54 . . .
Multiples of 9: 9, 18, 27, 36, 45, 54, 63, 72 . . .
Common multiples of 6 and 9 include 18, 36, and 54, but the least is 18.

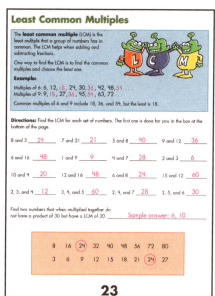

Directions: Find the LCM for each set of numbers. The first one is done for you in the box at the bottom of the page.

8 and 3 __24__   7 and 21 __21__   5 and 8 __40__   9 and 12 __36__

6 and 16 __48__   1 and 9 __9__   4 and 7 __28__   2 and 3 __6__

10 and 4 __20__   12 and 16 __48__   6 and 8 __24__   15 and 12 __60__

2, 3, and 4 __12__   3, 4, and 5 __60__   2, 4, and 7 __28__   3, 5, and 6 __30__

Find two numbers that when multiplied together do not have a product of 30 but have a LCM of 30. ___Sample answer: 6, 10___

8   16   (24)   32   40   48   56   72   80
3   6   9   (24)   15   18   21   (24)   27

23

The Factor and Multiple Trick

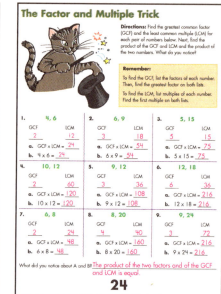

Directions: Find the greatest common factor (GCF) and the least common multiple (LCM) for each pair of numbers below. Next, find the product of the GCF and LCM and the product of the two numbers. What do you notice?

Remember:
To find the GCF, list the factors of each number. Then, find the greatest factor on both lists.
To find the LCM, list multiples of each number. Find the first one on both lists.

	1. 4, 6	**2.** 6, 9	**3.** 5, 15
	GCF LCM	GCF LCM	GCF LCM
	2 12	3 18	5 15
a.	GCF x LCM = 24	GCF x LCM = 54	GCF x LCM = 75
b.	4 x 6 = 24	6 x 9 = 54	5 x 15 = 75

	4. 10, 12	**5.** 9, 12	**6.** 12, 18
	GCF LCM	GCF LCM	GCF LCM
	2 60	3 36	6 36
a.	GCF x LCM = 120	GCF x LCM = 108	GCF x LCM = 216
b.	10 x 12 = 120	9 x 12 = 108	12 x 18 = 216

	7. 6, 8	**8.** 8, 20	**9.** 9, 24
	GCF LCM	GCF LCM	GCF LCM
	2 24	4 40	3 72
a.	GCF x LCM = 48	GCF x LCM = 160	GCF x LCM = 216
b.	6 x 8 = 48	8 x 20 = 160	9 x 24 = 216

What did you notice about A and B? _The product of the two factors and of the GCF and LCM is equal._

24

My Dear Aunt Sally

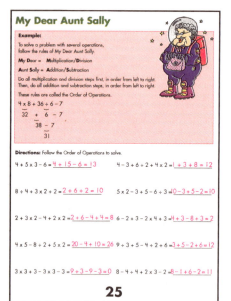

Example:
To solve a problem with several operations, follow the rules of My Dear Aunt Sally.

My Dear = Multiplication/Division
Aunt Sally = Addition/Subtraction

Do all multiplication and division steps first, in order from left to right. Then, do all addition and subtraction steps, in order from left to right.

These rules are called the Order of Operations.

4 x 8 + 36 ÷ 6 − 7
32 + 6 − 7
38 − 7
31

Directions: Follow the Order of Operations to solve.

4 + 5 x 3 − 6 = _4 + 15 − 6 = 13_   4 − 3 + 6 ÷ 2 + 4 x 2 = _1 + 3 + 8 = 12_

8 ÷ 4 + 3 x 2 + 2 = _2 + 6 + 2 = 10_   5 x 2 − 3 + 5 − 6 ÷ 3 = _10 − 3 + 5 − 2 = 10_

2 + 3 x 2 − 4 + 2 x 2 = _2 + 6 − 4 + 4 = 8_   6 − 2 + 3 − 2 x 4 + 3 = _4 + 3 − 8 + 3 = 2_

4 x 5 − 8 + 2 + 5 x 2 = _20 − 4 + 10 = 26_   9 + 3 + 5 − 4 + 2 + 6 = _3 + 5 − 2 + 2 + 6 = 12_

3 x 3 + 3 − 3 x 3 − 3 = _9 + 3 − 9 − 3 = 0_   8 − 4 + 4 x 2 x 3 − 2 = _8 − 1 + 6 − 2 = 11_

25

Exciting Exponents

Directions: When you see a figure like 5^2, the 2 is the exponent and the 5 is the base. This means that the 5 is multiplied by itself two times. Fill in the crossword with solutions written in word form.

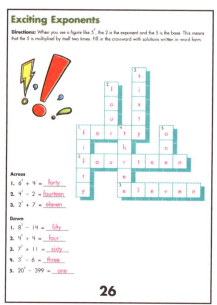

Across
1. 6^2 + 4 = _forty_
2. 4^2 − 2 = _fourteen_
3. 2^2 + 7 = _eleven_

Down
1. 8^2 − 14 = _fifty_
2. 4^2 ÷ 4 = _four_
3. 7^2 + 11 = _sixty_
4. 3^3 − 6 = _three_
5. 20^2 − 399 = _one_

26

Order of Operations Practice

Directions: Follow the order of operations to solve the number sentences below. Match each number sentence with its solution in the column on the right. Use the letters that correspond with each numbered problem to read the coded message.

_D_	1. 15 − (4 + 7)	**A.**	25
_O_	2. 5 x 2^3 − (27 − 21)	**B.**	2
_R_	3. 8 + 6 x 4 + 8 − 5	**C.**	52
_T_	4. 3^3 ÷ (3 x 3)	**D.**	4
_L_	5. 9 + 7 − 5 x 3 + 10	**E.**	168
_S_	6. 32 + 4 + 4 x 3	**F.**	19
_A_	7. 3 + 4^3 − 7 x 6	**G.**	100
_H_	8. 28 + (9^2 − 3) − 5 x 7	**H.**	9
_C_	9. 90 + 5 x 2 + 16	**I.**	89
_G_	10. 5^3 − 84 + 12 − (6 x 3)	**J.**	18
_E_	11. 98 ÷ (15 − 8) x 12	**K.**	43
_N_	12. 67 + 6^2 x 6 ÷ (2 + 1)	**L.**	11
_I_	13. 114 − 16 x 3 + 27 − 4	**M.**	38
_M_	14. 8^2 − (2 + 6 x 4)	**N.**	139
		O.	34
		P.	360
		Q.	317
		R.	6
		S.	20
		T.	3
		U.	36
		V.	98
		W.	10
		X.	206
		Y.	27
		Z.	32

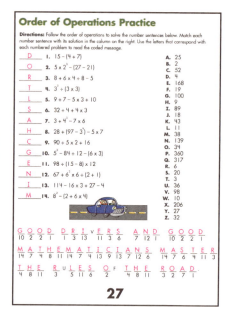

G O O D   D R I V E R S   A N D   G O O D
10 2 2 1   4 7 7 12 1   10 2 2 1

M A T H E M A T I C I A N S   M A S T E R
14 7 4 8 11 14 7 4 13 9 13 7 12 6   14 7 4 11 3

T H E   R U L E S   O F   T H E   R O A D.
4 8 11   3 5 11 6 2   34   4 8 11   3 2 7 1

27

Order Up!

Directions: Complete the equations below, making sure you follow the order of operations.

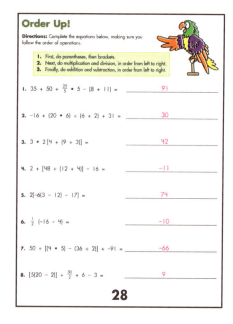

1. First, do parentheses, then brackets.
2. Next, do multiplication and division, in order from left to right.
3. Finally, do addition and subtraction, in order from left to right.

1. $35 + 50 + \frac{25}{5} \cdot 5 - (8 + 11) =$ _____91_____

2. $-16 + (20 \cdot 6) \div (6 + 2) + 31 =$ _____30_____

3. $3 \cdot 2[4 + (9 \div 3)] =$ _____42_____

4. $2 + [48 \div (12 + 4)] - 16 =$ _____−11_____

5. $2[-6(3 - 12) - 17] =$ _____74_____

6. $\frac{1}{2}(-16 - 4) =$ _____−10_____

7. $50 \div [(4 \cdot 5) - (36 \div 2)] + -91 =$ _____−66_____

8. $[5(20 - 2)] \div \frac{30}{2} + 6 - 3 =$ _____9_____

28